The ⎯ in the Mire

By Jenna Frandsen

ISBN: 979-8-218-31408-8

DEDICATION

To my mom and dad for raising me with unconditional love and with all the endurance in their bodies.

To Kyle, for supporting this part of my life as an open book.

To my children, may you always be a beacon of light in a, oftentimes, dark world.

123

The Meaning in the Mire

CONTENTS

The Meaning in the Mire

PRAYER

Dear God, take the hand of the one holding this book and surround them with the warmth of your peace. That they may know, in this moment, that there is hope in Christ.

"I do not know why we have the many trials that we have, but it is my personal feeling that the reward is so great, so eternal and everlasting, so joyful and beyond our understanding that in the day of reward, we may feel to say to our merciful, loving Father, 'Was that *all* that was required?'. I believe that if we could daily remember and recognize the depth of that love our Heavenly Father and our Savior have for us, we would be willing to do anything to be back in Their presence again, surrounded by Their love eternally. What will it matter…what we suffered here if, in the end, those trials are the very things which qualify us for eternal life and exaltation"

-    Sister Linda S. Reeves

The Meaning in the Mire

INTRODUCTION

In 2018 I had an impression that I needed to write down my story. I thought maybe it was to help me work through some bit of it I had missed. To move on from any part that was holding me back. To maybe just get it out of my head. I'm a huge believer in the therapy of putting pen to paper and just writing no matter the direction, theme, or desired outcome. But before I even started, I heard the distinct correction indicating the true purpose. It wasn't about me at all. It was about you.

In 2019 I still had not started but I knew the reason why. I didn't know "the how". Not only "how to start" or "how to end" and everything in between but the "what ifs" and "buts" kept creeping in. One morning I was watching the Today show and saw a woman who I had followed on social media who had overcome some real tough stuff and now continually makes people, like me, ugly laugh. Tiffany Jenkins was telling her story and message of life after addiction on the show and she said something about getting the motivation to write a book. To "just do it....start right now"[i]. So I did. That day.

As I sit here, in 2020, writing this, I come back to the present moment. I take my eyes off the page and look around. I see play clothes tossed around the living room, toys scattered around, tonight's dinner stuck to the dining room table. The exhaustion and the residual frustration from the day transforms into humble gratitude. I'm home. My heart is beating and it is full of love. Not only for those little people I love but for the love they give back to me. I shake my head. I cannot believe this is my life. Years of asking "aren't I doing enough?" has now become "what have I done right to be blessed like this?". The tally marks don't add up. And they never will.

This is how I know there is a God. Only a gracious God would bless me with not only life after what should have been my demise, but to be blessed with a family, a home and health.

That is truly poetic grace.

"And I will also ease the burdens which are put upon your shoulders, that even you cannot feel them upon your backs, even while you are in bondage;

and this will I do that ye may stand as witnesses for me hereafter, that ye may know of a surety that I, the Lord God, do visit my people in their afflictions."ii

This is my story and my testimony of that promise from our Lord and my promise to Him.

PREFACE

Addiction

The feelings the body goes through when needing its next fix is, what I imagine, the same feelings your body and brain go through when needing its next breath of oxygen. Suffocation. The panic that you feel as your brain is starving for oxygen, your body shaking from the inside out, your chest burning, is extremely intense. Horrific panic starts to build, eyes shifting as you wonder what comes next- your lungs filled with rejuvenating, life giving air, or the continued constriction of tissues, one by one, until you take your last breath. You need air. You need your drug. It is just as serious, as vital, and as desperate. It's as

6

if your mind doesn't know the difference. For all your mind and body knows, it IS suffocating. In that moment, you would do anything for air and you would do anything for a fix.

You may judge the addict, saying:

"Why do they do this to themselves?"

" Why don't they just get help?"

" Who would live like that?"

"Don't they see how they are hurting everyone else around them?

"Don't they care?"

The thought of purposely going through suffocation, knowingly going through that torture of the mind and body, knowingly breaking a law of the land, God's laws and sometimes the unwritten laws of familial bonds and loving relationships, and somehow getting on the other side of the withdrawal to work at staying clean and sober and righting all your wrongs and gaining trust and respect from others as well as yourself for the rest of your life, is sometimes more insane of a thought than actually staying in the madness of active addiction.

Using drugs is not glamorous. It is not fantastical. It is, however, a fast way to physical and spiritual death. The way out is up to you: By way of death, or, by the grace of God, the way to unbelievable spiritual, emotional and personal growth. But the choice is yours and I promise, either path is sure to bring you unimaginable pain, both physical and emotional. Mental anguish. It will take you places you never thought possible. You will be ripped from side to side and jerked around violently by the Adversary. The mental tug of war, the physical torture and the loss of the spirit is so great a feeling I can hardly put it into such words.

On one end of the rope I mentally I found myself in pieces. One piece that only thrives on that suffocating feeling- The rush of adrenaline that comes from dangerously living one day to the next on the excitement of no responsibility other than following your "friends" to the next party, getting a rush from another staggering drug high, taking you from the mundane to an out of this world state of ecstasy. Another piece that will go through anything, and I mean going to extreme measures you never thought you would, to get high. Showing up at a strangers (20 years older than you) backyard shed to "see what he's got", not before being patted down at the fence line. Or asking the person in the car next to you at the stoplight if he's got any "Coke", judging that since he just asked you for a cigarette, he might be open to helping you fill your void as well. After which you trustingly follow him and his friend to some unknowing neighborhood to get, not what you were looking for, but a new drug. Super. Driving your car home while under the influence- once believing I was in an actual video game and crashing into mailboxes and garbage cans was getting me "points". Filling your own home with toxic chemicals while innocent bystanders sleep in the next room. Or even sacrificing your God given, righteously intended, body as a pawn in someone else's game of exploitation to gain even the hope of another chance to get high. Another piece that is almost turned off of any humanity, because you have to. It's a reflex of survival. How can you allow your consciousness and gut instincts to appear in a "place like this?!". In that desperate and sickening state of defilement and desecration, the only correct choice here seems to be to turn off all humaneness that exists. However, the more practice you get doing such, that part of yourself might soon be very hard to get back. Another piece that is so hateful, angry, lonely, and bitter. You simply don't care what happens next.

The other end of the rope. The one being held by the Adversary. In his grip is the piece that is so small and far away, but still exists, it is that of the little girl or little boy that is scared beyond belief. She does not have a firm grip anymore. She is still holding on but it seems with little, childlike, fragile hands. She holds on through thoughts of her family. Their words and embraces. Memories of playing games around the dinner table. Laughing until you cry. Bowls of popcorn and chocolate covered peanuts. The smell of clean laundry and dinner cooking. Portraits of family and paintings of Christ on the walls. Holiday wreaths and music playing on the radio in the background. Memories of playing with nieces and nephews. Tickling their chubby thighs while laughing at their little giggles and feeling their love for you. Enjoying the hobbies you used to enjoy. Hiking up the canyon with just your dog and a camera. Cross Stitching with your mom while watching your favorite movie. Piano recitals, football games and family reunions. Your safe haven. It's funny how you live day to day without paying much attention to those details or just take them for granted.

That sweet spirit that longs to be held by their mother or father and desperately is seeking the light of Christ that she has lost. She is alone. In the utter darkness. A darkness so quiet and dense. Not the kind produced by the stillness of the Spirit, but a darkness so bitter and cold and frightening, that only the Devil himself can produce.

You're right. No one would ever **knowingly** create that or **willingly** stay in that life. THAT is why addiction is a disease.

Chapter 1

Born of goodly parents

I was brought up in a wonderful, happy home, consisting of game nights, family prayers, and lots of laughter. My parents never divorced, we all went to church every Sunday and remain very close to this day. I had lots of good influences in my friends and even in their parents! We moved many times during my childhood and teen years but I remember always in neighborhoods with friends, playing night games, basketball, Nintendo, riding bikes on dirt trails and trick or treating together.

As an adult, and especially a mother, I've wondered what led me to the choices I made growing up. Why I felt the need to self-harm, use drugs and alcohol, and not only live what became a destructive life but actually sought out that life and the people who lived the same way!

It never made sense to me. Two plus two didn't equal four. My childhood and the love I felt and experienced and always had around me didn't add up to the choices I made as a young teen up to my early twenties.

I could pretend to know why I did the things I did. The self-destructive behavior, the drug and alcohol abuse, the people I chose to surround myself with:

It could have been love. Yes, I was loved. Oh, I was loved! But my language wasn't spoken, so to speak, but maybe it was because it was hard to understand and because I felt that communication and understanding barrier, my tender heart began to feel less loved, including from myself. I began to feel like I was unable to be understood and in turn, maybe something was wrong with me. I began to hide those childlike attributes like creativity, self-expression, and outgoingness, that are so easily squashed by well meaning, but ignorant, teachers, parents, friends and adults.

Maybe it was a lack of communication. There was communication in my home but it was the communication between and parent and their child. Although loving, there was a barrier. It was communication between an adult and a child. There were boundaries, even if subconsciously, there were things you don't talk about until you're an adult or topics are kept in a corner until then because it was more comfortable to talk about or more appropriate to discuss or experience. If we had communicated then as we do now, as adults, I think things would have been a bit different. But to my parents' defense, I did need to do some growing up and gain natural maturity myself. And I know they tried to talk to the reluctant and embarrassed teen about sex, drugs and other topics that I would NOT listen to because it was awkward and I felt too vulnerable-which, to me, was as uncomfortable as being dipped in a vat of acid.

It could have just been my personality. I believe I was one of those children who are born with old souls. Those who are born in these little, limited bodies and their minds and spirits are beyond that of an infant! They feel more comfortable around adults, they are intellectual and creative, they seem to have brains that don't want to turn off. I was energetic and loved to have fun, especially if it was within the confines of my family and close friends. I wanted to be a part of everything that involved my family, especially exciting things and times where someone else felt loved and excited, like birthdays. I remember always wanting to be around my parents and their friends, listening to conversation, not wanting to just "go play with the kids". I would get offended easily when grownups (especially teachers) would talk AT me, correct me, tell me I couldn't do something. I hated hearing I couldn't do something because I "wasn't old enough" or because I was "just a child/teenager and won't understand until I was older". It would almost feel condescending and offensive or like I was growing and had potential

18

that was being stifled. That would upset me! And I acted out- maybe intentionally- but more unintentional. But I didn't understand it myself. I just felt like I must be "disobedient" and had an "attitude problem". I felt misunderstood, but really, I didn't understand me.

Maybe it was the chemical and physical rollercoaster that goes on with the mind and body as an adolescent. As I grew to be a pre-teen and teenager, I became more and more introverted and wanted to stay where I felt comfortable. I didn't like speaking or performing in front of others for piano, dance recitals or sports, but a part of me wanted to! What happened was something I think is common in adolescence, but we might not know why. I was losing my self-confidence and replaced that with self-doubt and low self-esteem. I refuse to believe that it is just "because I was a teenager". That is an excuse! As I look back at myself (even through home videos) I see that eight-year-old full of life and I think "There I am! What happened in between then and now?". Unintentionally, that spirit was silenced instead of being empowered (even by myself! I mean is there an instruction manual for a 15 year old to feel empowered and confident?!?). Now, in my Thirties, I feel like I fit in this world like a glove. Yes, I still love to hang out at the adult table now full of Sixty-five-year-olds, but I have never felt more comfortable in my skin and the world and company around me. I love it! It's like I've finally arrived. I'm not confused like I was growing up. Confused by why I couldn't be me and why I wasn't accepted. Confused by the myriad of directions my thoughts would go and working through the "this is what I want to do but what will they think" or "is it okay to feel this way about another person or about myself ?" or "Why did the teacher laugh at my comment?" Or "I really want to feel like I can tell my parents but there's no way!". It was like swimming against the current and the current being humans doing what they were always taught. Unfortunately, it was that closed minded, ignorant, go with the current of societies' way of raising children and treating others that caused that confusion in me.

Which brings me to the possibility it could have been the influential people in my life and their beliefs and their own insecurities. Specifically, being with the authority figures and teachers in my life. My years spent in the Young Women program was especially hard on me. How fragile a young person can be! This time of my life was crucial for developing my self-confidence and self-esteem. To be told that what you wear and how you act could "cause" another person to make wrong choices was the absolute, unequivocally, wrong way to teach kids. I will just say that I'm so happy with the awareness and the new Strength of Youth and the way most parents and teachers teach modesty, confidence and moral standards these days!

While I could write another book on the subject, could I just add a quick emphasis on shame for a moment? I'm not sure if Shame Culture is better or worse than when I was growing up, or maybe it's just different. I think a lot played into why I felt shamed in my life, one being my personality, another being the generation of my parents, friends' parents, and teachers grew up in, and another being just the choices and personal anxieties and insecurities of my church teachers and leaders. No matter who it was or what was said, it was always from a place of ignorance and not blatant hurt. Please watch not only what you say to a child but how you say it. It takes one *reaction* that sends the message of "what you're doing (or did) or thinking is shameful". That will turn that child away from ever wanting to come to you again. *Watch your reaction.* Just like when a baby is learning to walk and falls down and immediately looks to you on how to feel and react- if you look scared and say "oh no! Are you alright?!" or have a smile on your face and respond with "Yay! Get back up! You're doing great!" – their response corresponds! I feel as though there are so many hushed topics and scenes in the communities and religious groups we are apart of that are somewhat "molded" and when one steps outside the norm, everyone gasps at the thought of "what the neighbors might think". Oh, how I wish society would drop this habit! Now, I didn't say that what is wrong is wrong, and we should address when morals and standards are strayed from. If the law is broken, or adultery is committed, call it what is it – a hurtful sin! But, gosh, at the same time, it's also none of our business, is it? It's between that person and God. So don't call it anything, to anyone, unless it is YOU that is facing the sin. In that case, remember Repentance and Grace.

Never, not once, was it written that Christ felt ashamed by how someone acted or dressed. He never hesitated to offer service or His love in fear of what the "neighbors" thought. He handled those moments of addressing the one with shame of their sins, with compassion and disregard of what others might think of them after making their sins known.

He let them feel and know that He was only there for them. He was a protector and understood all. That rather than have a look of disappointment on His face (even with love), He would rather help them stand, and take that first step forward with them. That loving example is the one to strive for!

I think I longed for a comfort that I didn't know how to attain and every time I got burned by genuinely being myself, I finally threw my hands up. Burned by my ideas being shrugged off, my quirky childlike personality and behavior being seen as annoying, or my tender heart being criticized

then told to toughen up. There must be something

wrong with me. I was frustrated and sought

comfort. Comfort in the form of punishing myself,

seeking solitude and a "friend" of sorts and then

adrenaline, and chemical substances that

synthetically made me feel good about everything. I

wanted to either feel "something" or nothing. That's

the thing with addictions. The things that are going

on in your day to day life can trigger something

inside of an addict. Something that non-addicts

don't notice or maybe at least not to an unhealthy

degree. I think everyone likes rewards for a job well

done, a feeling of relaxing when life gets too busy.

But to an addict in a mundane state- we just want to

feel something (and use). When things are too much

to handle- we crave feeling *nothing* (and use or

"numb out").

What I thought was being free to be myself would

turn into completely losing who I was. And that

comfort I sought soon turned into a very

uncomfortable life.

The truth is, I don't know. I don't know why

I made the choices I did. I have thought about it in a

serious way, almost obsessively, for the last decade.

Especially since I've had my own children and with

the perspective I have now and seeing my own

children making their own decisions. The bottom

line is there are just so many factors that play into

the decisions you make as a human being and there

are so many different stages of life that influence

which way you choose to go and the choices you

make.

What I do know is- what matters is- the Lord is more interested in what we do in our trials and sins, how we come out of it, what our testimonies are on the other side, than the reason we did it in the first place.

Whatever it was, I was confused, alone and ashamed. All the while, not knowing why.

Chapter 2

Out of the darkness

How anyone claws their way out of active addiction is still beyond me. It is truly only by the grace of God that one who is finding themselves sinking in the quicksand of addiction, losing themselves inch by inch, with every step and struggle, tightening, panicking, suffocating, swallowed up until you think it's too late, is then effortlessly (if willing) pulled up toward the clean air and into the light where they are able to start breathing new life into their tired lungs. Effortless on Christ's part. Incredible willingness, faith, hard work and back breaking determination on your part.

Nevertheless, it is possible.

People have asked me "How did you get to where you are? How did you manage to get clean and sober?" May I share with you my experience of how I was led to the miracle of life after active addiction? I'm not going to beat around the bush. I'm not going to "whisper" about a taboo topic. Like I said, a life of addiction is not glamorous. It needs to be talked about in its raw form, unlike the picture the TV screen paints. It is dark. In one way or another, its life is dark. Don't allow the facade of the "cool" frat boy or giggling face of the beautiful girl at the party fool you. You never know what they might be going through behind closed doors or inside their own personal struggles that isn't talked about between groups of friends. And yes, there is something. I ask that you please, please, stay with me, as this is what is so beautiful!

The life giving Light of Christ is so much brighter after it is so dark.

It was December 31st, 2005. I had just got out of jail a few weeks before and was now in that place just before "rock bottom". Let's call it "the mud". It's that place where nobody is having fun anymore and you just hate yourself and what you've become. The place where you feel there is just no way back to the family that loves you, the safe shelter with the home you

grew up in or with the friends who used to call you for game nights. You are embarrassed and ashamed. You feel like you can't and shouldn't turn to any of those who love you for fear of judgment, repercussions, and end of relationships. You feel knocked off the social ladder as you are now a "huge burden on everyone" that is looked down on, or worse. I had just missed one of our favorite family Christmas traditions because I was sitting in a very cold (I hate being cold) jail cell eating fish sticks (I hate fish sticks) and being hung up on by every one I could remember the phone number for to call for bail. I had been put there sober. But I had told a lie to keep someone else out of jail for totaling MY car. And guess what, to this day I don't have a medal of honor for it. I do have a list of several jobs, however, that I didn't get because I now had a record.

Choose your heroic acts carefully.

My young 21 year old life was changing more and more. I was so tired of feeling weak. I constantly felt on the verge of death. My health was deteriorating and inside I felt so hopeless. Most of my days consisted of laying in a dark bedroom with hard music on my ears and the stench of not showering for who knows how long. Fun fact: I used to have aspirations of being a model in my teens, and now I'm too lazy to shower?! I was not able to see clearly through smoke and my own dull eyes. I thought: this is where it ends. I can't believe I'm here. This is it. I'm done. I had made sure I got enough Cocaine to ensure I did not wake up. Besides, I couldn't imagine going through the lengths I had to get more the next day. I was so tired of it. It was a chore. It was torture. Every time I showed up at another stranger's house, I really wasn't sure if I would make it back to my car that night or not. I used it. I used it all. No trace left.

My friends, what I am about to tell you is not from a hallucination or a dream or a nightmare. It was a blessing. The scariest blessing I've ever experienced.

Somewhere between this mortal Earth life of beauty and care given by a loving Heavenly Father, and leaving this life to enter a place of pure darkness and obsolete desolation, I saw a face. There was a face, not in my room in front of me, but in my mind and unconsciousness somehow. Not like a dream, that you remember after you wake up but as if you sat, sleepily in a completely darkened room, devoid of most of your senses but you are aware of its reality. It frightened me to my core. His eyes penetrated mine. He held my gaze and I knew pure evil at that moment. Then I heard him laugh. He was laughing at me. It was a demeaning and condescending laugh. I could hear him saying (not with my ears, but with my spirit), "You are a fool. I got you all this way and now I will watch you suffer. There is no one here for you. You fell for it.". I still remember the hollowness in my chest as I heard those words.

It is true what they say, that when you are dying, you really do see your whole life flash before your eyes. I saw my family and everything they encompassed and I felt just enough spark of light to hold onto it! Somehow, subconsciously or spiritually, I focused on that light and the strength from that love. My eyes flashed open and it was

morning. I don't remember much of the next few
days but I entered rehab on January 4th. Happy
New Year.

Chapter 3

Where is the hope?

Parents ask themselves "what can I do to help my child get sober?" It seems so obvious to the parent or the sober onlooker, doesn't it? Unfortunately, it takes hitting "rock bottom". Then the Earth quakes, and, as a result, the Earth cracks and they fall 100 more feet through heavy sludge and muck. They finally land in oblivion of desolate darkness, and, by the grace of God, they awake and take a step forward.

It wasn't the fear of my life ending-being a contestant in "life roulette"- that was that point for me. It wasn't sitting, very uncomfortably, in jail

feeling incredibly lonely, deserted and left
wondering how I had taken the steps to get there. It
wasn't the time that I was physically so broken I
couldn't even carry my weak, bloody body to a
shower that it took the charity of some dear friends
to do it for me. It wasn't even after suffering
through a sexual assault that left me feeling like two
people: a broken piece of the strong woman I
always hoped to be and a piece of an insignificant
shell of a human that deserved everything that was
being done to me and the many demeaning
experiences that took place many times after that.

It was seeing the face of Satan. Then the
strange but real sense of seeing my whole mortal
life, and seeing it from our Creator's eyes.
Especially the awareness that the things I had been
taught about the Preexistence, the Gospel of Jesus

Christ and His Plan, was indeed real. I couldn't deny it if I wanted to. It was that feeling of being so insignificant, yet beautiful, and small in this Great Plan. I was absolutely nothing to Satan. But because of the Light I felt in those dark times and the mere fact that I woke the next morning, I knew that I, little ole' me, was something to Christ. I knew I couldn't let Him down. I couldn't let anyone in my life that showed that Light to me, down. Heck, not even the smiling stranger I pass by going through the grocery store entrance! They deserved better, even if I didn't feel like I did. Eventually that Light grows bigger and bigger and you start to believe that even you deserve better from yourself.

It's what I refer to as a Spiritual Awakening. Find it. Chase it. Soak it up. For its power will move mountains.

Chapter 4

Rod of Iron

This part of the story might get a little frustrating for you (now you know how my loved ones felt). So stay with me and remember one thing: remember that mud and muck and how painful it was hitting bottom? You just stood up. You see worth inside yourself, even if it's just a small fraction. Don't discard it! Even when you might take a step back.

I finished three months in rehab, and I moved out and into my own apartment (mistake #1). I got a job (success #1). I was straddling between a healthy life I was trying to make for myself while looking for new friends and dabbling with old lifestyle habits. Can't have it both ways, friends!

Just like prison, there are certain steps and rules when coming out of Rehab. They are important, pay attention.

Here's where I need you to hang on. As a result of taking on the world as a "reborn rehab graduate" I started using again. This time I was using, what I like to call a "faster approach to rock bottom". Not for long, for I quickly, and thankfully realized I was going back down faster and quicker than ever before. Let me tell you something, when even the guy who supplies you drugs doesn't want to hang out with you or tells you to stop, it's time to get a grip.

I'm telling you this part of my story because relapse is a real thing. It can happen because overcoming addiction is more than hard work. It is a daily habit of practicing self love, self awareness, and contact with a Higher Power and even then, it's not a certain promise that you will stay clean and sober that day. That is why it is important for you, the loved one of an addict, to stay put. Be that "Rod of Iron" for someone! Whatever that may look like! It is important for you, the one with an addiction, to remember that rod. Whatever it may be (family, a good friend, the Gospel, your kids, AA meetings) and DO. NOT. LET. GO. No matter what. If you take one hand off and relapse, you keep your eye on it and grab it once again and **move forward**. Now, this doesn't give you the game instructions to have it both ways. Remember, that doesn't work. Trust me and every other addict and alcoholic sitting in meetings! You never know what life will hand you.

It might blow a gust of wind and it might throw a catastrophic tornado at you and you can't seem to hold on no matter how much you want to. It is absolutely imperative that you remember your Rod of Iron.

Chapter 5

My Catastrophic Tornado

From the first time I can remember, romance was in the stars for me. I wasn't the "boy crazy" girl, I was "the one" boy, idealistic girl. I never wanted to date around. I wanted to find "the one"- probably the day after I turned Nine. I planned my first boy/girl party for shortly after I turned fourteen. I fantasized about graduating from high school and shortly after that getting married and having babies. Lots and lots of darling, giggling, perfect babies. Everything would be perfect. My husband would love me unconditionally, be a strong member of the Church and of society and we'd smile and laugh constantly.

Plan all you want, have goals and aspirations! But remember two things, you have your agency, and God has a plan of His own.

Hi, I'm Jenna, and I had expectations that crashed and burned.

I was in a long-term relationship in my late teens/early twenties that was a defining hinge point in my life. During this relationship I was still trying to find who I was becoming as I was entering adulthood. I was stuck in that awkward age of life of dressing to impress and doing what I could to "be cool". And that might have meant staying out late when I really just wanted to be home, to going to a movie that made me feel uncomfortable but didn't want to be the "lame friend", to going to parties with immature, rude college kids and trying to remember my stance on drinking alcohol. I still hadn't found my voice and that was clear.

My boyfriend was a good man. We had so much fun and I still have a special place for him in my heart as a dear friend. There were times, though, I remember getting my feelings hurt, deeply hurt and I wouldn't say or do anything. Instead, I would get in my car and drive to a grocery store parking lot between our two houses and sob. I remember so vividly my stomach in pain and strained from the emotional hurt I felt and the physical strain from crying. It was my character and spirit that was hurt over and over. My self-esteem and self-love was disintegrating like tissue of the once strong heart and spirit that was born 19 years earlier. Over those years it had, bit by bit, got weaker and began to break apart. By the end of that relationship, it was bruised and truly tattered. I could not stand up for myself.

I was tired of being hurt and not fitting into this world and its mold. I couldn't figure out how to stop getting hurt by just being me. Note to self: It was because I was trying to be someone I wasn't. If you seem to be hitting a wall in life, self check- are you trying to go against the grain of who you feel you are inside? It's ok if you haven't figured just who you are in this life yet, keep loving yourself and you'll figure it out faster than most.

Somehow I had subconsciously made a

decision and started to change. I hushed the real person inside and decided to become who I thought was easier to be- a more worldly person that was more accepted. I had immediately lost my humanity of sorts and put up a shield that would protect me from being hurt anymore. I felt my spirit being pushed down further to protect it and the compassion in my eyes left. I decided to embrace the hurt. Feed the fire. I couldn't fight against it anymore.

A few years earlier I had caught the eye of a friend's brother. I paid no attention as he was older than I was and I had a boyfriend. But I knew his hard background and I knew he'd be the one to help me self-destruct. So I started flirting with the possibility, and him. What was at first playfully experimenting with matches, so to speak, quickly became a fuel to my bonfire. I was on a road I couldn't turn back around from. I knew I had chosen a life that was not easily forgiven and by the time I realized that, I was in love and I was addicted. Torn between two worlds. One world was one that I knew I could make a life of- make a family and rise above! The other had my throat in the vice of addiction. And that was it.

We continued the path of wanting to grow together, better ourselves and make a life that was worth living. And not being able to stop using long enough to breathe some life into us. We went to AA meetings, although not many, and the time I went drunk was the last time I went. He still held a full time job, I could not. Despite loving my teaching job and doing something I always wanted to do, I couldn't stay clean, not even in class. I would stop right in the middle of assisting in a class and go to the bathroom to get high. I couldn't even go forty five minutes. That was November. December I was in jail. And you remember how I spent my New Years.

Remember those "getting out of rehab" rules I referred to? Getting out and getting engaged was pretty against those rules. Getting out and getting engaged to the man you used with was VERY frowned upon to say the least. Although some family and friends were leery about this decision (and some down right against it) we moved to a home together. I had gotten another job at a hospital that I loved and had a real passion for (still do!). We had cleaned up our lives, were enjoying family activities, and were attending classes to prepare to go to the LDS Temple. We still had our regular marriage setbacks and standard arguments, but we were happy and had goals. We worked hard to remind each other of the things that keep us clean and sober and watched each other's backs. It seemed like when one of us was weak, the other was strong. And so this continued. It was tough on our relationship and it was real life hard work but we were healthier and stronger than ever before.

This is where that God given gift of agency can get

tricky

\

The time I heard the words "they found him, they found his body" was the worst moment of my entire life. Those words still seem incoherent to me even now, thirteen years later. They are almost funny. Not "ha ha" funny but unreal, surreal, and unfathomable. Not the meaning of them that day, but the insane psychological, emotional and physical storm that took place within my body upon hearing only words.

My husband was working out of town on a job that week. He sometimes traveled three, four, five hours away but mostly was around our hometown and this job was only an hour and a half away and to a city we'd been to a million times. No biggie. Nothing out of the ordinary. He was even working with family!

Before I went to bed that night we talked on

the phone. Just about our day that day, what the next day had in store- him going off to work and me getting his five year old son out the door to Kindergarten. The last two things we said to each other are words I will never forget. I told him I missed him and remember saying "are you just going to bed now?". I remember that simple question so well because the answer that came after it was a lie. And the last thing I

remember saying to each other – in that phone call and in our mortal lives- was "I love you".

The next morning I got a call saying that he hadn't shown up for work. Everyone he was staying with at the hotel had shown up, including his brother. That is when I knew something was wrong. I immediately got in the car and drove with family members to the hotel where he was staying in Salt

Lake City. We talked to the front desk, asked about cameras and about the people staying there. We called his phone and the police, and now scraping the bottom of the desperate barrel, I made the eerily paralyzing call to the hospitals and then morgues. You never know what that call feels like until you are doing it. I instantly felt like all the moments in my life had led up to this one. That my life's camera was zooming in on me and all music and rational thinking had stopped. I couldn't have heard my own heartbeat if I had wanted. It was as if I were alone in a gigantic tin barrel, running out of air. I *thought* it was the worst thing I could be doing at that moment. But it got worse. After getting zero answers or cooperation from anyone, I decided to get in my car and go looking for myself. I walked out of the front door of the hotel to my car and I'll never forget the details of the scene. I felt so

confused, confused at why nobody else was as

frantic as I was. Confused that nobody seemed to

know anything. I thought, Wasn't there people with

him?! Didn't anyone see him leave? Wasn't anything

out of the ordinary? Why isn't anyone telling me

anything?!. And then, as I looked north, up the

street, there was one, single person on the sidewalk

walking toward me. We locked eyes, a block and a

half away. I watched as he stopped in his tracks,

turned around, and ran out of sight. I knew three

things right then: that man was the only one who

had the answers I needed, this wasn't going to end

well, and I would never see that man again.

I got into my car, on a mission, and before I

could pull away from the curb, I saw my mother in

law come out of the hotel, her hand holding a

phone, moving in a confused manner from her ear, out to me. She was shaking her head and crying. I flew out of the car and started demanding "What happened? What happened?!"

His body was found. Abandoned. As if it hadn't belonged to a loving family, a warm home and memories past and hopes for the future. My knees buckled and I fell to the ground. Screaming so long and so hard I lost the ability to swallow. I felt my chest cave in, burning with such intensity that as my spirit watched my body breaking down, I felt excited that this sensation might actually take me too. That is the moment. That is what I see over and over again. Every detail down to the feel of the concrete beneath my hands. Watching through searing tears, my saliva hitting the tops of my fingers. Instantly feeling drained and all energy and life force gone, I felt exhausted and could have curled up right there as if it were my own bed. Then just as suddenly, adrenaline kicked in and I jumped up and ran to my car. I tore away from the curb and drove. Drove while my mind raced. I didn't know where I was going or what I was doing. Maybe if I got home and started the day over it would erase what had just happened. Maybe if I drove fast enough my adrenaline would subside and things will feel better. Or maybe my heart will just stop and this will be over. I would go in and out of moments of rational thinking like:

What am I going to do now?

I have to plan a funeral.

I need to contact family.

What just happened?!

Oh my gosh, what has happened?! My love. My

love.

Maybe they're wrong. Maybe it wasn't him! I have to go back! How could I be so stupid?! Of course! There is hope.

Let me tell you, it took approximately five or so years to get out of the habit, the real delusion, that he was not actually gone. There were times I would look over in traffic and think: What if he's out there?. I would fantasize about running into him. Finding out he's still alive. I had a recurring nightmare for years after that I was looking for him and could never find him. When I finally did he was just nonchalantly going about his life. I was so hurt and would ask him why he's acting like this, why he made the decisions he did and why he left. And he would just stare at me blankly. It was truly a nightmare that haunted me during waking hours for years and years.

I now know that that was the Adversary.

Compassion of the Lord

You see, there are two perspectives: One from the Adversary who says "He obviously didn't care about you. Why would he? He had an addiction, which took him down in the end. And so do you. And you, too, will not win against it. Give up now."

Another, from the sweet Lord that embraces you and says "Oh, my dear child, my sweet child. I'm so sorry. The struggles you have gone through. The decision that he made was his and even up until the last moment of his life, he thought of love and felt despair."

I was blessed with an experience about nine

years after his death. An experience I hold very sacred. I will tell you that I was blessed to know and feel and see those last moments my husband experienced. I will tell you now, my friends, he was not alone. He did not hurt but felt overwhelming peace and forgiveness. At the time of this experience, my heart was healed and I went on to not have another nightmare but a few very spiritual dreams that brought more understanding and peace.

Do not misunderstand my point. This doesn't mean his work of repentance is over! It just means that even in the midst of your transgressions, you are allowed peace.

My dear husband had demons. Some small and some very damaging and dangerous. But, let me tell you, his sweet spirit and good heart never changed. It was always there. As it is. That's what

I'm trying to tell you. Your spirit is always in there.

You just have to remember how to access it, honor

it and use it's strength.

Chapter 6

That Spirit Inside

Following his death, I could not function. I would sit, expressionless, day after day. I would cry so much for so long that it took, and I'm not kidding, a good couple of years to cry again. I always say that it is because I ran out of tears.

After the numbness I had felt after his passing wore off, I couldn't bear the thought of living without him. I hated waking up every day. Reliving the moments of finding out about his death. Reliving the reality of my new life without him. I could not bare this new life. I decided not to. The result of that decision was an overdose. In the moments immediately following that overdose, I remember not being able to get my eyes to focus, I would blink hard again and again and I would see things. Things I knew weren't actually there. The room looked distorted. I knew my brain was being damaged and it scared me. I grabbed for a pen to write but I couldn't hold a pen. I was so weak. I was so frightened.

And then things were very clear.

Let me stop right here. This is the first poetic point to my story and our lives. I was locked inside my own torture, barely physically able to lift a small pen! Hearing my healthy, rational mind making sense of what was happening yet knowing what my body and brain were experiencing as the repercussions of overdosing myself. Back and forth, back and forth. Spinning and sick. Clawing. And in the thick of it, instantly, my eyes were clear. The spinning stopped. I felt scared, alone and wanted the comfort of my childhood bedroom, my mother and the feeling of love.

You see, it is here that you realize that it is Satan that has a literal death grip on you. His hand is wrapped so tightly around your throat, squeezing and squeezing, until you can't hold a pen or a thought in your head. You realize, oddly in this moment, that the Gospel is true. That the stories are true. Again, that I am just a small piece of this great Plan. You gasp as you feel the Spirit and the light it brings. That minuscule crack of light. That moment that you feel the conviction of the Lord's mercy and unconditional love for you is so powerful that it can make even the most excruciating tormented life feel hope.

But it's too late. I start to panic that I've made a mistake and grab the nearby pen and paper and just write "I'm sorry. I'm scared. I'm sorry". I know I only have a few seconds before it's over. I run (actually walking very slowly) upstairs to where I know my dad is. The last thing I remember is answering his question of "Jenna, what did you do?" and it's black. I ended up going into a grand mal seizure. Then an ambulance ride to the ER, where I had another one, and then another on my way to the ICU. Not before receiving a Priesthood blessing which kept me out of said ICU. During my recovery I continued to have pretty heavy hallucinations and oddly I have a pretty good memory of the events (which, I believe, is meant to be a blessing).

Shortly after returning back home I moved

into a new apartment to get away from all the thoughts and memories (Addicts tend to run, cover up, self-medicate instead of dealing- if you haven't caught on to that pattern yet). I got a part time temporary job, where my dad worked, but that didn't stop me from dreamily walking into my Dad's office and just falling to the floor in sobs, unable to finish my shift.

I missed my husband so much. I didn't understand why this was happening. I just felt so terribly hopeless and stuck, every day.

I turned to alcohol to numb the excruciating pain that waited for me every morning. Before I even put my glasses on, I would grab a bottle. Despite knowing that the Lord was aware of me, I knew it- why would I still be here?, I would cry to my mom saying "I have no faith left. I don't know why I'm still here. I don't know how my heart hasn't just stopped. Why am I going through this?" I didn't know why this was happening. I waited and waited for an answer. But the longer I waited, the more my faith would diminish.

In hindsight I was not very patient, but I had no faith, let alone works! But we don't see that until down the road, after the lesson, right? Imagine how we'll look back and feel after this life is over!

But I had to hold on to the glimmer of that spirit still inside me. I had seen it again that day before I blacked out. The spirit I had seen that New Years Eve.

There it was. Grab it. Hold on to it.

It's a decision. Make it or continue to struggle. Life is a test. But it is not hard. The moment it gets to the point of skidding on your face through life, forcing things to happen only to get overwhelmed and frustrated, stressed and tired- you have officially gotten off the paved (sometimes made of dirt instead of beautifully paved, nevertheless, it's still clearly marked) path God laid out for you. So, make a decision. What do you want? Get up. Get going.

Chapter 7

Decisions, Decisions

I'd read an inspirational book entitled "Jesus Calling" by Sarah Young. There is a theme I've noticed. Many daily quotes and guidance from Christ say the overall message of "Stop trying to avoid difficulties in life, that is precisely where I want you. They bring you closer to Me"[iii].

While Christ is always interested in our joys, the things that bring us joy, and the joys we take to others, He is more interested, I think, in what we do when we are in difficult circumstances. Whether it be our life decisions that have brought on sadness or pain. Or times like watching a child make wrong choices, a neighbor suffering a loss, or a friend going through a divorce. What do we do in those times? How many times have you seen that friend throw their hands up and say "Who cares!" Or have that child leave the house mid-argument and proceed with a slamming door. Or in the heartbreaking decisions of a loved one who, through their weakening tears, say "I'm done".

Our friends and family may decide that the sometimes difficult task of following the commandments or guidelines of the Gospel are "too hard", "not worth it", or they just don't understand "why" and they leave the church or succumb to their addiction or another equally destructive decision.

I heard a story once about two friends, two young men. One a son who didn't have a testimony of the Gospel anymore and didn't follow the commandments because they were "too restrictive" and didn't feel like he had any freedom. The second was a returned missionary, a good kid, who made one bad decision and had pre-martial sex with a young girl. She shortly afterward decided to make a decision of her own and instead of explaining to her parents the mistake she had made, decided to tell them it was rape. This young returned missionary is now facing ten years in jail for breaking a commandment given, by inspiration, from the Lord. THAT is your freedom taken away! We make mistakes! There is **no** perfection in this life. Thank goodness! The way I see it, this is an example of what to do now...now that this young man is in a very, very difficult time in his young life, what is he going to do now? Blame the Lord for the commandment, blame the scared girl for her wrong decision and the injustice of the situation, hate the laws of the land, or hand it over, seek for humility and strength from the Lord?

It is a decision. It simply is.

Before you say "well it's easier said than done" or "if you were in that position, it might not be what you would do", think of a few things: The hell you just read and where I'm sitting now or better yet, the story of Mary Magdalene[iv], the faith crisis that Joseph Smith went through at times throughout the entire Doctrine and Covenants[v] or the best story of all- the story of Jesus Christ, His pleading with the Father, even to the point of asking for relief, and His ultimate suffering in the end.[vi]

Injustice? Depends on who you ask and the perspective you have.

Trust

I've heard a lot of parents talking about their

teenagers making maybe not so righteous choices.

The teenager then says "you just don't trust me!"

and the parent says "you're right, I

don't". Let me tell you that when I heard that, I

unexpectedly felt a 'ping' in my chest. I heard that

a few times in my own teen-hood. I hadn't realized

how much that impacted me. At the time it impacted

me in a way that I only can look back now and

understand more fully. I believe that upon hearing

that from a parent, it immediately made me feel

insignificant and caused a loss of respect. Now you

might be thinking "Well that's just immature" or

slightly laugh it off, but don't. That's a mistake that

happens often I think. It might not *seem* like a big

deal and it might not be to your child! But if it IS your child, it IS a big deal.

Let me offer a perspective. Imagine if you've gone throughout your life, as a "regular" human, making mistakes, going through trials, etc. You've had your share of humble realizations and have gotten down on your knees for forgiveness many times. Repented. Begged the Lord to give you "one more chance!" Let's make this even more of a serious transgression- much more than breaking curfew. You've done something so seemingly terrible you can barely look at yourself in the mirror. You can feel the shame set deep in your bones. Humility is a hard emotion to practice. But you know what's right and you know what steps to take. You know what you need to do as a human being, as a Christian, to move on. You pray. You pray and talk to your Father with the humility of a little child with a broken heart and a need to feel forgiveness and warmth from a loving parent...and the Lord says to you "I'm sorry, I just don't trust you. I can't trust you. I'm disappointed". Now that feeling IS bone set.

What is the truth? The truth is we don't trust *Satan*. We don't trust him when our children are infants. We don't trust him when we are Fourteen and getting straight A's. We don't trust him as adults living "by the book". He can catch us off guard at any moment of our lifeline. At ANY phase of life or circumstance. Let alone the vulnerable times!

We *need* to be able to trust ourselves! Teenagers *need* to be assured over and over and over that they can trust themselves! They can trust the spirit inside themselves! That is something that some don't learn until adulthood, or sometimes never at all!

Let's change the dialogue:

"Do you not trust me?!"

"Yes. I trust you. I trust the warrior inside of you. I trust the testimony (knowingly or unknowingly) inside you. I trust your kindness and intent. I will never trust Satan. And unfortunately, it doesn't matter if the more you let your light shine outward or the weaker you feel, the harder Satan will work on you. Not only do I trust you, I am counting on you. Strangers are counting on you. The Lord is counting on you. And you are never alone in the fight."

Let me go back a bit. When I referred to a

teenager making a "not so righteous decision" in my recent example, I want to, if I can be so bold, clarify what I define as "righteous". When I say "righteous choices", I feel like that is a stereotypical blanket statement. I want to break this down. What I mean is: broke a Commandment, defiled a sacred ordinance, purposely and maliciously hurt someone, broke a *serious* law of the land, or really cannot answer "yes" to all or feel good about the temple recommend questions. What I do **not** mean: broke the law by going ten over the speed limit set up *by the law*, came in later than curfew, hasn't gotten good grades and isn't really trying, doesn't seem to care about household chores, stays on his or her phone or video games for hours at a time, talked back disrespectfully, played with friends on Sunday, wore

jeans to church, didn't participate in Family Home
Evening. I could go on.

Please do not misunderstand me. The
children (we are **all** children!) who have been guilty
of the above are one thing- sweet children with
sweet spirits that feel misunderstood. And that
may manifest into anger-even rage, depression,
unsympathetic behavior, uncompassion, and
more.

Just as Jesus turned the water into wine,
filling more than enough vessels to the desperates'
plea[vii], He has given us more than we need. We are
the ones who make life more difficult than it needs
to be. He wants us to have joy!

Imagine when your children get into a spat.
You advise them to make amends and apologize for
hurting the other. I like to go one step further and

ask them to give each other a hug. Immediately

their shoulders drop, their mouths curve up into a

smile, and the energy has shifted into a beautiful

moment. Touch releases the chemicals Dopamine

and Oxytocin and lowers Cortisol- the stress

hormone. So even in difficult moments, we are

allowed, encouraged and able to turn them into joy!

To bask in the energy, excitedly given by God, of

joy. But it takes humility. It takes feeling

uncomfortable for a moment. Sometimes very

uncomfortable! But in return, we are filled with the

feeling of peace and gratitude that can only be

obtained and offered by and through pure Deity.

So, it is a choice. Will you humble yourself

enough to ask for help or forgiveness? Make the

changes and choices necessary? Take action?! Even

if it means to go against what your friends are doing

or makes you stand out uncomfortably while being judged by friends, members, neighbors and even family. Are you ready to be blanketed with the warmth of the Almighty and receive the strength of a thousand oxen to push forward, to take the next right step? Or will you grit your teeth, bitterly cry that "there is no way!" you can go on or submit yourself that way. No matter the reason! It may be because it will cause too much discomfort going to parents to come clean and receive the repercussions. Going in front of the judge, to ask for reprieve. To a loved one. Or to God to ask for one more chance.

If you find the humility, don't forget the Grace.

Chapter 8

Looking back through these stories, the moments that left a scar of conviction on my heart and in my testimony were the moments when I realized God's Grace. The perspective we are given in an exact moment is a gift from God. It is one of those moments that hit us deep and for a moment we see the truth with our spiritual eyes. For a moment we are unshaken, unbroken and absolutely sure.

Hold on to that moment for as long as you can. Write it down. Share it. So you never forget it. For it will carry you through to the end of this life and very possibly through the trials that you, or someone else will face. God is gifting you that moment for a divine purpose. Recognize it! THAT. That is what this life is all about.

His Grace

So what is my purpose, or I should say what is God's purpose for having me write this book? It is to talk about the simple beauty of this Earth life. And His grace that carries us through it.

Things happen in life. These things have happened to me. And as much as I don't like to think about it, I know hard times may still lie ahead. I don't like saying "hard times are inevitable" because it gives me an "impending doom" feeling like something is going to happen at any second. In fact, let me talk about this for a moment if I can.

I've struggled in life, holding on to the joy

there is in the world instead of getting swallowed up in the news stories that there is only despair, corruption, poverty, sickness, rebellion, and hatred. Having had the experiences I've had with seeing drug and alcohol abuse, physical and sexual abuse, choices of friends or family members and my own consequences of seemingly innocent "time of the teenager" choices but that effectively led to destructive choices later, I have adopted a mentality that "these things just happen". They happen to everyone and it is inevitable. As I started having my own children I've worried about this from the time I saw that second pink line. I hear words in my head like:

Enjoy their innocence now for it will be gone one day.

Teach them now before it's too late.

Shield them, scare them straight, no- approach this topic with love and the gospel...but that is how I was taught and look at the choices I made! Ah! I don't know how to raise children in this day! We're doomed to a life of trauma, abuse and loss.

Wow, ok, that's dramatic and maybe a little irrational...but these are the thoughts that penetrate my heart and mind every single day. I have been working hard to rewire my brain and way of thinking and I hope I can help you too.

Going back to that "impending doom" feeling, I know that if I keep hold of the perspective that the Lord has given me from these experiences, and also the promises within my Patriarchal Blessing, I can have the confidence and the faith that I have the tools to survive and endure with joy, whatever may come.

Men are, that they *might* have JOY

So how do we endure with joy and remember His Grace?

First- I remember what I feel at every General Conference. That is when I see the faces of the Prophet and General Authorities. Their expressions are full of the Spirit and true joy and I feel relief. When I hear them say they aren't worried, I'm not worried. They smile, I smile. They have hope for the future of this world and that the generation being born now are THE children who will lead the world to God. Not only do I sustain their words with the true conviction I feel but my heart swells from the Spirit bearing witness to me (little old ME, that I take to the Lord every day) that He promised me that *joy* is one of THE purposes of this life. We aren't to just repeat this scripture in our

86

heads now, during times of trial, but that we *will* have joy with Him later, or, even later in this earth life, always living in the future, hoping for something better. Yes, we will have joy later, with Him. But His intention for us is that we find joy in this life, now. He's provided us with joyful things!

Here's the key word, though, *might*. "Adam fell that men *might* be; and men are, that they *might* have joy"[viii]. We have a choice. I'm not saying that we can't really feel the pain and disappointment we're feeling, or the fear and worry. We know the source of fear and we know the source of pure joy. I have learned (and continue, daily, to remind myself) that in these experiences, it is better to have the companionship of the Lord than wish to be alone or seek the companionship of a bitter feeling, gut wrenching worry, or the illusion of companionship of addictions (refer back to Chapter 4 on making

that decision).

Second: Seek the Light of Christ. This

current time on Earth is full of stories, experiences,

and events that fill us with sadness, uncertainty,

faith crushing worry and debilitating fear. Some of

these terrible things are coming to us from the

outside in. The TV, internet, stories of a friend of a

friend. But some of these things could be within our

own homes or happening to us personally. If I

would have written this ten years ago I would have

said something like "We all have deaths in the

family, mental illness, addictions, that shut that light

down". But after my sister married her husband and

I learned that he had never seen anyone close to him

pass away (including, until recently, his great

grandparents!). He has also had no history of mental

illness, no family members in prison for robbery or drugs. I was perplexed and drawn to this enigma! No, this apparently was just a norm in my own family. I don't want to assume, but for the sake of this point I'm going to say "We all have felt impenetrable darkness".

How do we keep the faith?

How do we hold on to that light, The Light of Christ??

Today it seems like there is more darkness, destruction, terrorism, and evil. But remember the many stories in the scriptures of the hateful mobs, illness and famine, natural disasters, murder, and faith crisis.

Take the brothers of Jared for example. There was such evil in their world that the Lord punished them by making them unable to

understand each other when they spoke. Think
about that. Wouldn't it feel isolating and lonely to
not be able to communicate? That would feel
like darkness. But because of his prayers to the Lord
and his faith in the Lord he was led and he
was blessed with his family and given direction that
would lead them to peace. Along with hard work
(even work with seemingly no end or reason),
seeking physically and mentally, they were blessed
with literal light for their boats.[ix] Remember,
though, not before Christ asked the brother of Jared
to think about what he could do to create light in the
barges. This is an example of doing "all he can
do"[x].

Then it says, "And thus they were driven
forth; and no monster of the sea could break them,
neither whale that could mar them; and they did

have light continually, whether it was above the water or under the water."[xi] The way I read this was that we have the light of Christ when our head is above water and we can see the blue skies and feel the warmth of the sun. And we can also have the light of Christ when we are drowning, in the darkness, feeling alone, and feeling the desperate despair that we can find ourselves in.

David Butler recently said in another awesome "Don't Miss This" podcast that he was so humbled by the fact that someone in the scriptures, who by the way, doesn't even have a name mentioned, could be so blessed by the Lord! That made him feel like even when you feel insignificant or maybe not worthy in a way, that the Lord is aware of even you. Aware even of a man called the "Brother of" someone else in the scriptures![xii]

Six times in the Doctrine and Covenants, Jesus said, "I am the light and the life of the world, a light which shineth in darkness, and the darkness comprehendeth it not."[xiii]. I love that it uses such a powerful word. It doesn't say "and the darkness goes away" but "the darkness <u>comprehendeth</u> it not". That means no matter how hard it tries, the darkness cannot put out that light. Ever. You can trust that His light will be there for you. Which brings me to the third way to endure with Joy, and that is remembering His grace[xiv]:

The Lord tells those paralyzed with grief: "I will...ease the burdens which are put upon your shoulders, that even you cannot feel them upon your backs **even while you are in bondage** that ye may know of a surety that I, the Lord God, do visit my people in their afflictions."[xv]

To those who are just so tired, Jesus assures us to "Come unto me, all ye that labour and are heavy laden, and I will give you rest"[xvi]

To those who feel like they just don't fit the traditional mold, remember that Jesus made great efforts to reach out to all kinds of people including lepers, children, Galileans, harlots, Pharisees, sinners, Samaritans, widows, Roman soldiers, adulterers, and the ritually unclean. In almost every story, He is reaching someone who wasn't traditionally accepted in society.

To those who have question upon question, remember, this is not the stage in our eternal development where we have all answers. It is the stage where we develop our assurance (or sometimes our hope) in the evidence of things not seen. Remember that this is not a complicated gospel. Keep it simple. Jesus said, "I am the light, and the life, and the truth of the world."[xvii]

And to those who feel like they can never be good enough, Brad Wilcox 's talk titled "His Grace is sufficient" is one of my favorites. He says something I've always remembered. "Too many are giving up on the Church because they are tired of constantly feeling like they are falling short. They have tried in the past, but they always feel like they are just not good enough. They

don't understand grace."[xviii]

Carrying the light with you it doesn't mean these certain times will be easy. It doesn't mean you still aren't human and have bad days. I'm sure despite the light, the people of Jared had plenty of scares in the depths of the sea, illness beyond empathy, times of lacking faith and begging for reprieve. But they came out OK. Not perfect. But more faithful and praised by God for their patience, effort and humility.

Seek for stories of strength and love, choose to see the good news. Above all, serve. It's the quickest way "out of yourself". Try it. You'll see.

God has not abandoned us and He does hear our prayers. "The Savior has reminded us that he has graven us upon the palms of His hands. Consider the incomprehensible cost of the Atonement and crucifixion. I promise you He is not going to turn His back on us now."[xix] In this

dispiriting trial and depressing time that you may

find yourself or your pleading with the Lord for the

suffering of a loved one as was the Prophet Joseph,

the voice of God comes saying "My Son, peace be

unto thy soul. Thine adversities and thine afflictions

shall be but a small moment. And then, if thou

endure it well God shall exhaust thee on high; thou

shalt triumph over all thy foes"[xx]

Please don't abandon Him.

Please don't abandon yourself.

Please don't abandon those you love.

Chapter 9

**"The Family that prays together, stays together"-
a humble fridge magnet[xxi]**

I had a turning point while I was in rehab. I remember my mom sending me quotes, scriptures, and LDS Living magazines. I'll never forget that. It seems so insignificant but it wasn't. I had read what my mom had given me, every day. Even when I didn't want to or thought it wouldn't help. I remember praying regularly...but I don't remember prayers that weren't along the lines of "God help me to not die today. Be with me. I'm sorry".

This night was different. I had gotten on my

knees and through sobs, I prayed. I prayed so hard

inside my head and heart that I couldn't contain it

silently anymore and prayed out loud. Begging for

direction and comfort. Pleading with the Lord to

hear my prayers. I opened my eyes. I grabbed my

scriptures and opened them to a random page,

pointed, looked down and read:

"And my soul hungered; and I knelt down before

my Maker, and I cried unto him in mighty prayer

and supplication for mine own soul; and all the day

long did I cry unto him; yea, and when the night

came I did still raise my voice high that it reached

the heavens."[xxii]

My chest immediately became sunken with

an ache and butterflies. I knew the Lord heard me. I

was elated. I felt loved. I felt seen. And then I felt

humbled. In the way that if Christ himself stood

before me, I would be silenced, dumbfounded, I would buckle and I would be

brought to my knees in respect and reverence. I wept like a small child and felt as if I was wrapped up in the warm embrace of my mother.

A Plea for Parents

Mothers- don't stop telling your children how valued they are. How beautiful they are. How much the Lord loves them. Don't stop sending them texts with uplifting quotes, thoughts and smiley faces. Don't think that taping up seemingly cheesy one line messages or affirmations on the mirror of your teenagers is a lame idea. It isn't. And you're not wasting your time. Even if you are flat out told by an eye rolling teen that it is.

Fathers- don't stop having high expectations

for your child, as long as it is met with high love for them. Never hesitate to answer the phone no matter how upset you might be that the rules were broken, once again. If you must bite (hard) your tongue the whole ride back from picking them up (or bailing them out), do it. Because if the previous advice is taken, they'll *know* you expected better but love them no matter what and they will be feeling the bitter heartache of disappointing you for years to come. Lastly, don't stop showing them that they have a loving home, no matter how long and hard their time away from it is.

Because one day, maybe two, ten, or forty years down the road, that same child might find themselves at a crossroads between a decision that will keep them on the path of righteousness and a decision that will tear them apart. A night out with friends that is getting later and farther away from home and the feelings of homesickness are creeping up. Or, worse, a situation that makes them think "how did I get here, and how do I get back?" and that one, lame saying you had stuck to the fridge all their lives will pop back in their heads and might just be the one thing that pushes them to make the better choice, gives them comfort, or brings them back from hell.

When they hit their rock bottom, no matter what they may look like, or if they feel like they have no home or no one to love them, they will remember where they once felt the love and safety of a home, and return.

Don't give up hope. When there seems to be none and inside you now feels like tattered piece of cloth that was once a strong flag of your faith, remember that the Lord never leaves us. Whether we are taken from this earth, or we are saved through the grace of God. I am a witness of that on two accounts in my own personal life, not recounting those from the scriptures, that even when you find yourself staring Satan in the eye from a sinful decision or you cross that veil from this life to the next (from a sinful decision), the Lord is with you.

Rationally, how can you have hope when your loved one (or yourself!) seems so far gone? So consumed by darkness and ensnared by Satan's barbed wire, that you wonder if you will ever see the light again.

Remember:

"My soul hath been redeemed from the **gall of**

bitterness and bonds of iniquity. I was in the *darkest* abyss; but now I behold the marvelous light of God. My soul was *racked with* eternal *torment*; but I am snatched, and my soul is pained no more."[xxiii]

If you are the one struggling with a demon- Don't give up. Climb. Claw your way out and toward that light. I promise you what's waiting on the other side are blessings you never thought possible. I KNOW it is hard. Hard doesn't even describe it. I know it is anguish and I also promise that it will take every thought, every breath and every bit of strength you have to do it. However, you must do it, do it! Fake it til you make it if you must. I know it seems so much easier to not climb, especially when you might be so physically weak.

But you are not alone. I pray for you every day.

Pray for yourself. Those on the other side of the veil

ARE there holding you up. Remember your Rod of

Iron. Focus on it. Let it lift you up until you can

hold yourself up and then hold others up, because

you will be a force to be reckoned with! Charity

prevents a multitude of sins![xxiv] It will keep you

above water.

I want to give you a thought to keep with

you and to help you as it has helped me in those

moments of weakness and mental torment. It is to

do the next right thing and then the next and then

the next. Play it out. Play out the scenario that you

are about to embark on. How does it end? I know

it's hard to see the end of a horror movie if you've

never seen it, but you can guess. Just do the next

right thing and if you can't find the strength, hit your knees and don't move! You can't go far on your knees and chances are if you're on your knees, you'll be willing to PRAY. Prayers can sound like many things. You pray the prayer that comes out. Sometimes that just comes out as tears and incoherent words. That's alright. God knows exactly what you're telling him. May He be with you as you keep moving forward- with BOTH feet.

If you are the one struggling with watching a loved one suffer silently- Don't give up. Keep encouraging. Be a companion, and a safety net while not enabling. Do it **together**, but not **for** them. Keep praying. Pray for them. Pray for yourself. Keep loving. Fill your cup! Keep your strength up by taking care of yourself. I know watching a loved one suffer brings your health down quickly. It's not selfish, it's a fact. Take care of yourself. Love yourself. Time is wasted by giving yourself a guilt trip, telling yourself you could have done better at this or that, "shoulda, coulda, woulda" (this takes practice and faking it sometimes!). Allow yourself Grace.

Remember the roots that keep you stable and unshaken. The roots that you came from or the roots that you plant. Stay strong. Be firm. Know who you are and what you're capable of through the Atonement of Christ.

"..*after ye have gotten into this strait and narrow path, I would ask if all is done? Behold, I say unto you, Nay; for ye have not come thus far save it were by the word of Christ with unshaken*

faith in him, relying wholly upon the merits of him

who is mighty to save.

Wherefore, ye must press forward with a

steadfastness in Christ, having a perfect brightness

of hope, and a love of God and of all men.

Wherefore, if ye shall press forward, feasting upon

the word of Christ, and endure to the end, behold,

thus saith the Father: Ye shall have eternal life. "xxv

"For this is hope of a tree, if it be cut be cut down,

that it will sprout again, and that the tender

branch thereof will not cease. Though the root

thereof wax old in the earth, and the stock thereof

die in the ground; Yet through the scent of water it

will bud, and bring forth boughs like a plant "xxvi

If you are struggling with addiction, please reach out to your nearest Alcoholics Anonymous fellowship or go to http://aa.org or http://na.org. Talk to an LDS Bishop about LDS Recovery Services.

If you are the loved one needing a support group please reach out to a member of your local Al-Anon group or visit http://al-anon.org

If you are thinking of ending your life and need a lifeline, please call 988 or go to 988lifeline.org

REFERENCES

[i] Tiffany Jenkins, Today Show, NBC, June 2019

[ii] Mosiah 24:15; Book of Mormon

[iii] "Jesus Calling"; Sarah Young, Thomas Nelson, 2004

[iv] Luke 8:2, Bible, KJV

[v] Doctrine and Covenants

[vi] Matt. 26:36, 39; Mark 14:32; John 18:1, Bible, KJV
Alma 21:9; D&C 19:15-19, Book of Mormon
Matt. 27:22-50; Mark 15:22-37; Luke 23:26-46; John 19:17-30, Bible, KJV

[vii] John 2:1-11, Bible KJV

[viii] 2 Nephi 2:25, Book of Mormon

[ix] Ether 1-6 Book of Mormon

[x] 2Nephi 25:23, James 2:14-26 Book of Mormon

[xi] Ether 6:10

[xii] "Don't Miss This", David Butler, YouTube,Nov 9-15, 2020

[xiii] D&C 10:58, 34:2, 39:2, 45:7, 6:21, 88:49, YouTube, Nov 9-15, 2020

111

[xiv] Apart from Sharon Eubank, "Christ: The Light That Shines in Darkness", General Conference, April 8, 2019; D&C 88

[xv] Mosiah 24:15 Book of Mormon

[xvi] Matthew 11:28 Bible KJV

[xvii] Ether 4:12, "Jesus Christ, Light of the World"- Topical Guide

[xviii] Brad Wilcox, "His Grace is Sufficient", June 7, 2012 BYU Devotional

[xix] Jeffrey R Holland, "Broken Things to Mend", General Conference April 2006

[xx] D&C 121:7-8 Doctrine and Covenants

[xxi] Al Scalpone, 1947, "Family Theater" National Radio Program

[xxii] Enos 1:4 Book of Mormon

[xxiii] Mosiah 27:29 Book of Mormon

[xxiv] 1 Peter 4:6 Bible KJV

[xxv] 2 Nephi 31:19-20 Book of Mormon

[xxvi] Job 14 Bible KJV

14853675R00076